STAR WARS
THE MANDALORIAN

The Adventures of Din Djarin

DK	Elinor De La Torre, Sarah Williams,
Senior Editor Matt Jones	Jackey Cabrera, Nick Miano, Allison Bird,
Project Art Editor Stefan Georgiou	and Michael Trobiani
Production Editor Marc Staples	**Photographers** François Duhamel, Nicola
Senior Production Controller Mary Slater	Goode, Justin Lubin, and Melinda Sue Gordon
Managing Editor Emma Grange	
Managing Art Editor Vicky Short	DK would like to thank Chelsea Alon at
Publishing Director Mark Searle	Disney; and Julia March and Kayla Dugger for proofreading.

Reading Consultant Barbara Marinak

For Lucasfilm
Editor Jennifer Pooley
Creative Director, Publishing
Michael Siglain
Art Director Troy Alders
Story Group Leland Chee, Pablo Hidalgo, and Kate Izquierdo
Creative Art Manager Phil Szostak
Asset Management Chris Argyropoulos, Gabrielle Levenson, Bryce Pinkos,

First American Edition, 2024
Published in the United States by
DK Publishing
1745 Broadway, 20th Floor, New York,
NY 10019

Page design copyright © 2024
Dorling Kindersley Limited
DK, a Division of Penguin
Random House LLC

© & TM 2024 LUCASFILM LTD

24 25 26 27 28 10 9 8 7 6 5 4 3 2 1
001–337851–Jan/2024

All rights reserved.
Without limiting the rights under the copyright reserved above, no part of this publication may be reproduced, stored in or introduced into a retrieval system, or transmitted, in any form, or by any means (electronic, mechanical, photocopying, recording, or otherwise), without the prior written permission of the copyright owner. Published in Great Britain by Dorling Kindersley Limited

A catalog record for this book
is available from the Library of Congress.
ISBN 978-0-7440-9217-2 (Paperback)
ISBN 978-0-7440-9218-9 (Hardcover)

DK books are available at special discounts when purchased
in bulk for sales promotions, premiums, fund-raising, or educational use.
For details, contact: DK Publishing Special Markets,
1745 Broadway, 20th Floor, New York, NY 10019
SpecialSales@dk.com

Printed and bound in China

www.dk.com
www.starwars.com

This book was made with Forest Stewardship Council™ certified paper—one small step in DK's commitment to a sustainable future. For more information go to www.dk.com/our-green-pledge

Level 3

The Adventures of Din Djarin

Written by Matt Jones

Contents

6	Meet Din Djarin
8	What is a Mandalorian?
10	Din Djarin's armor
12	What is a bounty hunter?
14	The galaxy
16	The *Razor Crest*
18	Grogu
20	The Armorer
22	Mudhorn
24	A clan of two
26	Din Djarin's allies
28	Greef Karga
30	IG-11
32	Peli Motto
34	Din Djarin's Naboo N-1 starfighter

36 Boba Fett
38 R5-D4
40 Moff Gideon
42 Bo-Katan Kryze
44 New adventures
46 Glossary
47 Index
48 Quiz

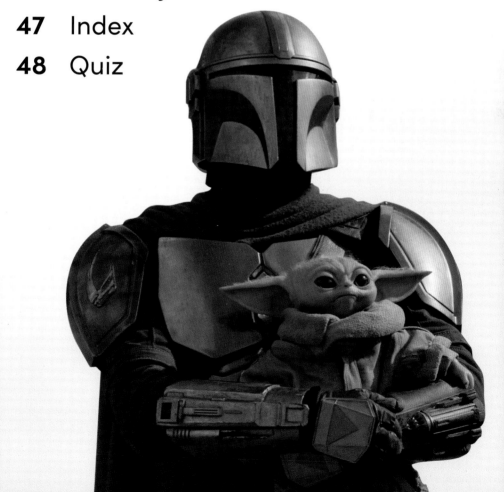

Meet Din Djarin

Din Djarin is a Mandalorian bounty hunter. He is very brave and looks after his friends. Din Djarin goes on many adventures. Din Djarin looks after his son, Grogu.

Grogu

What is a Mandalorian?

Mandalorians are a group of people who come from the planet Mandalore. They are famous for being powerful warriors. Most Mandalorians wear suits of armor. Some Mandalorians disagree on what rules are important to follow as a Mandalorian.

9

Din Djarin's armor

Din Djarin's suit of armor protects him. It has many built-in gadgets such as a flamethrower and a jetpack. His suit is made of a special metal called beskar. This metal is very rare. Beskar only comes from the planet Mandalore.

What is a bounty hunter?

Bounty hunters are paid to track people down across the galaxy. Some bounty hunters are members of the Bounty Hunters Guild. Bounty hunters often find themselves in dangerous situations.

Cad Bane

The galaxy

A galaxy is a group of stars and planets. Din Djarin lives in a big galaxy that is far, far away. Din Djarin visits many different planets on his adventures.

Tatooine

Mandalore

The *Razor Crest*

The *Razor Crest* is Din Djarin's starship. He pilots the starship around the galaxy. The ship has a cockpit, a cargo hold, a bedroom, and even a toilet!

Engine

Cockpit

Grogu

Grogu is Din Djarin's adopted son. Grogu is 50 years old, but he is still a child. His species takes a long time to grow up! Grogu can use the Force to do many amazing things. He can heal wounds and jump really high into the air.

Grogu uses a hover pram to move around.

The Armorer

The Armorer is a smart Mandalorian. She is very skilled at making Mandalorian weapons and armor.
The Armorer is an important member of the Children of the Watch.
The Children of the Watch are a group of Mandalorians. They believe that they should never take their helmets off in front of others. Din Djarin is also a member of the Children of the Watch.

Mudhorn

The mudhorn is a species of creature found on the planet Arvala-7. Each mudhorn has a single large horn on their head. Mudhorns use these horns to dig nests into the muddy canyons of Arvala-7. Din Djarin and Grogu defeat a mudhorn on the desert planet.

Din Djarin is holding a mudhorn egg.

Mudhorn

A clan of two

The Armorer decides that Din Djarin can start his own Mandalorian clan. A Mandalorian clan is a small group of Mandalorians that are like a family. The Armorer names Din Djarin's clan after the mudhorn creature. Din Djarin and Grogu become members of Clan Mudhorn.

Din Djarin's allies

Din Djarin visits many worlds and makes many allies. Kuiil is an expert at fixing droids and vehicles. Fennec Shand and Koska Reeves are great in battle. Carson Teva is a skilled starfighter pilot.

Kuiil

Fennec Shand

Koska Reeves

Carson Teva

Greef Karga

Greef Karga used to lead the Bounty Hunters Guild on the planet Nevarro. Now Greef is the high magistrate of that world. A high magistrate looks after a planet and the people who live there. Din Djarin and Greef are very good friends. Greef likes to give presents to Grogu.

IG-11

IG-11 is one of Din Djarin's allies. He is a droid. IG-11 likes to care for and protect others. IG-11 saves his friends from being captured on the planet Nevarro, but he is badly damaged. Din Djarin finds the parts needed to repair IG-11. The droid then starts working again and decides to help protect Nevarro.

Peli Motto

Peli Motto is a mechanic. She lives in a city called Mos Eisley on the planet Tatooine. She runs a docking bay where ships can park and be repaired. Peli is good friends with Din Djarin and Grogu. She helps Din Djarin find a new ship after the *Razor Crest* is destroyed.

Din Djarin's Naboo N-1 starfighter

The *Razor Crest* is destroyed, so Din Djarin needs a new starship. Din Djarin buys an N-1 starfighter from Peli Motto. She helps Din Djarin repair the ship. These shiny ships are created on the planet Naboo. Din Djarin's N-1 starfighter can fly very fast. Grogu really enjoys the speedy ship!

Engine

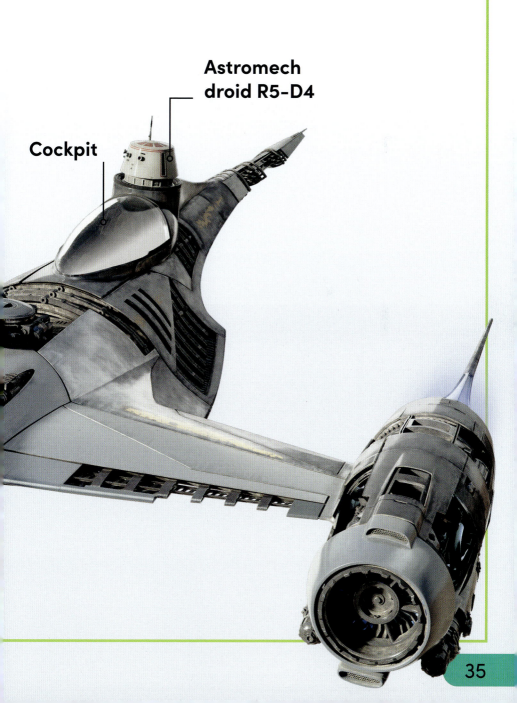

Cockpit

Astromech droid R5-D4

Boba Fett

Boba Fett is a bounty hunter. He wears Mandalorian armor made of beskar. Boba's armor was stolen, but Din Djarin finds it and returns it to him. Boba and Din Djarin help each other out.

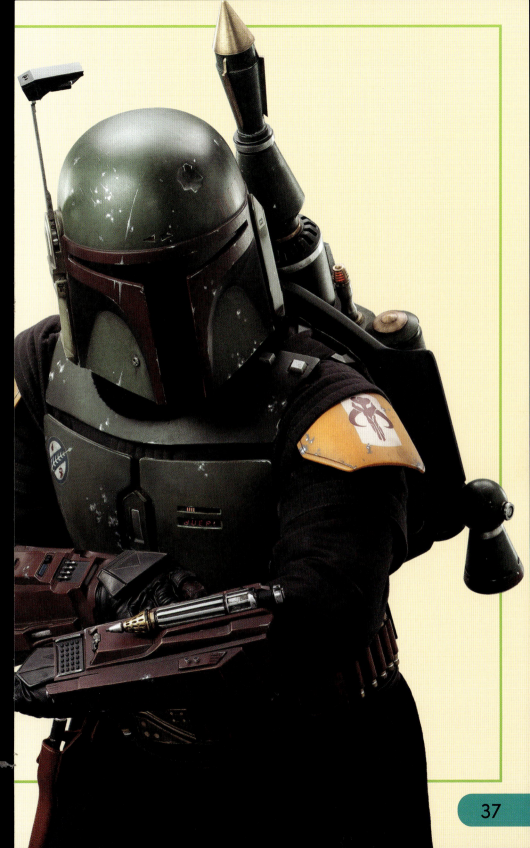

R5-D4

R5-D4 is an astromech droid. He knows starfighter pilot Carson Teva. R5-D4 now works for Din Djarin. The droid flies with Din Djarin in his N-1 starfighter.
R5-D4 visits Mandalore with Din Djarin and is very helpful and brave.

Moff Gideon

Moff Gideon is a tough leader. He defeated Mandalore's leader, Bo-Katan Kryze, and took over the planet. Many Mandalorians do not like Moff Gideon. Moff Gideon decides to kidnap Grogu. Luckily, Din Djarin comes to the rescue and saves Grogu. Moff Gideon has a secret base on Mandalore.

Bo-Katan Kryze

Bo-Katan Kryze used to rule over Mandalore, but Moff Gideon forced her to leave her home. She helps Din Djarin and Grogu on the planet Trask. Din Djarin and Grogu then help her defeat Moff Gideon and destroy his base on Mandalore.

Bo-Katan, Din Djarin, and Grogu are good friends.

New adventures

After Bo-Katan Kryze defeats Moff Gideon, the Mandalorians can return to Mandalore. Din Djarin decides to start protecting others. Din Djarin and Grogu then visit

their ally Greef Karga on Nevarro. Greef gives them a cabin to live in between missions. Din Djarin and Grogu's adventures are not over yet!

Glossary

allies
people who help another person when they need it

astromech
an astromech droid is a type of droid that helps people travel around the galaxy

Bounty Hunters Guild
a group of bounty hunters who follow a number of rules

cabin
a type of house that is often small

cargo hold
a part of a vehicle from where items can be packed away

cockpit
a part of a starship where the pilot can control the vehicle

creature
another word for an animal

droid
another word for a robot

hover pram
a type of vehicle that can fly in the air and carries infants

mechanic
a person who helps build and repair machines

species
a type of living thing

starfighter
a type of starship often used in battle

starship
a type of vehicle that can travel in space

Index

armor 8, 10–11, 20, 36
Armorer, the 20–21, 24
Arvala-7 15, 22
astromech 35, 38
beskar 10, 36
Bo-Katan Kryze 40, 42–43, 44
Boba Fett 36–37
bounty hunter 6, 12–13, 28, 36
Cad Bane 12
Carson Teva 26–27, 38
Children of the Watch 20–21
droid 26, 30, 35, 38
Fennec Shand 26–27
Force, the 18
galaxy, the 12, 14–15, 16

Greef Karga 28–29, 44
Grogu 6, 18–19, 22, 24, 28, 32, 34, 40, 42, 44
IG-11 30–31
Koska Reeves 26–27
Krrsantan 13
Kuiil 26–27
Mandalore 8, 10, 14, 38, 40, 42, 44
Mandalorians 6, 8–9, 20, 24, 36, 40, 44
Moff Gideon 40–41, 42, 44
mudhorn 22–23, 24

Naboo N-1 starfighter 34–35, 38
Nevarro 15, 28, 30, 44
Peli Motto 32–33, 34
R5-D4 35, 38–39
Razor Crest, the 16–17, 32, 34
Riot Mar 13
Tatooine 14, 32
Trask 15, 42

47

Quiz

What have you learned about Din Djarin and his allies?

1. Who is Din Djarin's son?

2. Where does beskar come from?

3. Is the Armorer a Mandalorian?

4. R5-D4 is not an astromech droid. True or false?

5. Who helps Din Djarin on the planet Trask?

1. Grogu 2. Mandalore 3. Yes 4. False 5. Bo-Katan Kryze